DK ESSENTIAL MANAGERS

GW00602607

Globalisation

SARAH POWELL & PERVEZ GHAURI

London, New York,
Munich, Melbourne, Delhi

Senior Editor Peter Jones
Senior Art Editor Helen Spencer
Executive Managing Editor Adèle Hayward
Managing Art Editor Kat Mead
Art Director Peter Luff
Publisher Stephanie Jackson
Production Editor Ben Marcus
Production Controller Hema Gohil

Produced for Dorling Kindersley Limited by

cobaltid

The Stables, Wood Farm, Deopham Road,
Attleborough, Norfolk NR17 1AJ
www.cobaltid.co.uk

Editors Louise Abbott, Kati Dye,
Maddy King, Marek Walisiewicz
Designers Darren Bland, Claire Dale,
Paul Reid, Annika Skoog, Lloyd Tilbury

First published in 2008 by
Dorling Kindersley Limited
80 Strand
London WC2R 0RL
A Penguin Company

A CIP catalogue record for this book
is available from the British Library.

ISBN 978-1-4053-3154-8

Colour reproduction by
Colourscan, Singapore
Printed in China by WKT

See our complete catalogue at

www.dk.com

Contents

Introduction

The world economy is being reshaped by a process of change that offers enormous opportunities and substantial threats to many businesses. Understanding globalisation, its drivers and implications, is key to recognizing and responding to today's new business pressures. Ignoring it is not an option in a world in which the opening of markets and easing of restrictions on foreign direct investment have hugely increased competitive pressures.

Globalisation offers a snapshot view of the history, drivers, and challenges of this process. Its information and advice will help managers to understand and take practical steps to address the enormous and rapid changes that are taking place – changes that affect every aspect of business life from communication and location to sourcing, manufacturing, servicing, distribution, marketing, and human resources. Armed with this knowledge, companies can more confidently pursue the many opportunities opening up to them.

The World Bank predicts that the global economy could expand from $35 trillion in 2005 to $72 trillion in 2030. To be successful, businesses need to be ever more aware of market forces, ever more competitive, ever more agile and rapid in adapting to change. The potential benefits of globalisation for business and society are enormous – as are the risks and the responsibilities. This book provides the information you need to guide you and your business to a successful global future.

Chapter 1

Understanding globalisation

Globalisation may be the dominant economic trend of our age, yet the urge to travel and trade has been as important to human history as that to invade and conquer. The history of global economic interaction holds valuable lessons for business today.

Defining "globalisation"

The term "globalisation" is most commonly used today to refer to a specific economic phenomenon – the emergence, in the 1980s, of a single world market, dominated by multinational companies and characterized by the free flow of private capital across borders.

Deregulating markets

Globalisation became a buzzword in the late 20th century because this was an era that saw a rapid and massive expansion in international trade and investment – enthusiastically taken up by business and the media. The main agent of the change was widespread deregulation – the removal by governments of anti-competitive measures, such as price controls, in key markets around the world. As corporations, goods, services, and capital began to cross borders, consumers' growing aspirations and involvement in financial markets added momentum.

Dividing opinion

Trickle-down effect — *hotly debated theory that incentivizing high earners encourages them to work harder, leading to job creation that benefits low or non-earners. The counterclaim is that only the already-wealthy benefit.*

The positive interpretation of the word "globalisation", or its early equivalent "Americanization" – reflecting US global power and influence – primarily denoted a process of opening-up of commercial and investment opportunities in new and often distant markets, leading to economic integration. Proponents of this positive view claimed that there would be a "trickle-down effect"* by which capital would filter down from rich to poor countries – and thus lead to a fairer, more democratic and peaceful world.

Opponents of globalisation, however, warn that it reduces the ability of nation states to control their economies. They also raise ethical objections to the exploitation of developing markets and the imposition of Western values on indigenous cultures.

Buying the global product

Multinational — *a business that manages production establishments or delivers services in at least two countries. The UN also uses the word "transnational" for companies with assets outside their own countries.*

Whatever the interpretation, for the consumer globalisation increasingly means that an everyday product – a television set, say – might be designed in one country, manufactured in another using materials or components sourced from a third, marketed through a call centre in a fourth, for delivery and use in any number of others. As such, labels of "origin" have clearly lost their meaning.

For business, the opportunities are unprecedented. UN estimates for 1990 showed some 35,000 multinational* corporations with 150,000 foreign affiliates, and total stock of foreign direct investment worldwide of $1.7 trillion. Today there are believed to be some 60,000 such corporations. However, not all multinationals are big businesses. As new technology and management innovations promote entrepreneurial agility over size, a new size of multinational – the "micro-multinational" – has emerged.

The earliest global traders

The evolution of today's global market economy can be traced back to the emergence of the first inter-regional trade routes, markets, and migrations, developing through the creation of powerful regional empires, some of which lasted for hundreds, if not thousands of years.

Forging early trading links

Well before 2000 BCE traders in high-status goods covered the huge distances between Mesopotamia (modern Iraq) and India. The centuries from 1600 to 600 BCE were characterized by power struggles for control of Syria, which lay at the junction of trade routes east to Mesopotamia, westwards to Asia Minor and the Aegean, and south to Egypt. These early attempts at empire-building were to be replicated over the centuries in many parts of the world, creating political and military superpowers that united previously disparate kingdoms.

Building the first empires

The first great empire, China, emerged in 221 BCE, lasting for some 2,000 years. Under the Han dynasty China traded silk and jade across caravan routes to Siberia, India, Persia, and the Mediterranean. Over the centuries other empires emerged, reshaping the regions of the world. In the 1st century BCE Rome succeeded Greece as the dominant power of the Mediterranean, forging an empire that at its height covered most of Europe and North Africa, with trading links as far as China and India, the Baltic, and Ireland.

Combining military might and economic power, these early empires were characterized by a high degree of central authority; many, for example, imposed a shared currency across their territories. The impulse to spread religious philosophies – notably Buddhism, Christianity, and, from the 7th century CE, Islam – was also a spur to expansion. Up until about 1350 the economies of both Christian Europe and the Islamic Middle East were boosted by African gold.

Exporting the market economy

A major leap forward in the evolution of global trading came at the beginning of the 16th century, when power shifted decisively toward western Europe. Technical advances in navigation, exploited notably by Portugal, signalled the "Age of Discovery". Underpinned by military might and financial institutions – in particular the emerging Italian banking system – Europe's maritime expansion, like the early empires, encompassed trade but also proselytising, slavery, and colonization. Western empires subsequently covered much of America, Africa, Australia, and India – spreading the concept of capitalist market economies*. When its empire was at its height, Britain alone among European nations ruled over a quarter of the world.

*Capitalist market economy — *an economic system in which the means of production are all or mostly privately owned and operated for profit or capital.*

 IN FOCUS...

THE FIRST MULTINATIONALS?

Founded in 1600, the British East India Company provides an early global business model. It had its own private army, acquired substantial territories, and established trading stations in Surat, Madras, Bombay, and Calcutta, exchanging bullion, lead, quicksilver, and woollens for calico, diamonds, drugs, porcelain, saltpetre, silk, and spices. The Dutch also had an East India Company, which built up a virtual monopoly in European trade in the most prized spices, and was the first company in the world to issue stock.

Creating mass markets

For global trade in goods to prosper, several needs must be met. First, there must be a supply of goods surplus to the needs of a domestic market; second, demand for those goods in foreign markets; and third, a transport infrastructure capable of delivering goods from manufacturer to consumer.

Revolutionizing industry

The earliest industries were coal, iron, and textiles. The Industrial Revolution took root in the early 19th century in the north of England, Germany, Belgium, and Wales. The water-powered spinning frame, steam-powered weaving loom, electric motor and generator, and steam railway were among inventions that were to reshape business, trade, and industry. Industrialization spread east and north across Europe, extending to Siberia and the Near and Far East with the introduction of rail and canal networks.

During this period, the US economy was enjoying massive growth, boosted by the population growth resulting from immigration and the transportation opportunities opened up by the newly built railroads. By the end of the 19th century the US rail network was more extensive than that of all Europe, including Britain and Russia.

A new superpower

Building on the skills of its entrepreneurs and immigrants, the settlement of new land, investment from Europe, and an unequalled transport infrastructure, by the early 20th century the US had become the world's richest country. The defeat of Germany in the First World War was to establish its economic might on a global scale.

The costs of the war on all countries involved were huge but it was particularly damaging to European nations that had been at the heart of the conflict. European and worldwide trade and markets dramatically declined. The US took on the role of global financial centre and embarked on a programme of foreign direct investment. Its finance capitalism can be seen as a modern version of the earliest forms of empire-building. This, in addition to its size and thriving domestic economy, ensured its role as a global power.

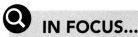

IN FOCUS...
THE BIRTH OF CONSUMERISM

The US was the world's first consumer society, with mass marketing bringing products once reserved for the rich within reach of those of more modest means. Sears, Roebuck pioneered mail-order sales in 1891, at first offering watches, then sewing machines, bicycles, prams, ovens, cheap refrigerators, and many other products, at enticingly affordable prices. The American market drew far ahead of the rest of the world in terms of household comforts and appliances. US innovation, sales, marketing, and advertising talent was later exported with early products including Coca-Cola® (launched in the 1880s and first exported in 1926), Frigidaire (launched 1918, exported 1920s), and Hoover (1908, exported 1919) – all of which became generic names. "Coca-Cola" is said to be the most widely recognized term in the world after "OK".

The emergence of global business theory

Many of the first management operations theories arose from within early 20th century industry in the US, and in particular in the automobile industry. They provide a fascinating study in the spread of global production and management techniques, as well as consumer aspirations.

Fordism and mass production

Production-line manufacturing was first introduced in the US in 1902 at the Oldsmobile car factory. By 1913 Henry Ford had developed conveyor-belt assembly for his Model T range. Ford's new production system assigned workers to specific locations on the production chain, where they worked continuously and repetitively. This led to both higher output and fewer accidents. This new, very efficient and profitable way of working, called "Fordism", was soon adopted by other US industries.

 IN FOCUS... TAYLORISM

In the early 20th century, Frederick Winslow Taylor, a US engineer and inventor in the steel industry, conducted studies prompted by his interest in efficiency that explored the best way to perform a manual task by timing its component parts. His findings led to huge gains in productivity and his work was the forerunner of modern time and motion studies. His theories, which became known as "Taylorism", and also as "scientific management" because they sought to analyze operating processes, still inform cost-efficiency ideas. The modern practice of outsourcing – assigning stages in production to the most cost-efficient location – has been called "Taylorism for the 21st century".

Expanding into world markets

Mass production led to Ford seeking ever larger markets, and it exported from its earliest days. Ford also built a network of franchised dealerships, in order to ensure consistency of standards of service as well as product wherever Ford cars were sold. In 1911 Ford began manufacturing in the UK and France. A decade later it expanded into Denmark, Germany, and Austria and, in 1925, into Australia. Local manufacturers soon adopted "Fordism".

Sloanism – the first global model

By the 1920s Ford was the dominant automobile brand. Yet within three years General Motors (GM) was to become the country's leading automobile company, under the stewardship of Alfred P. Sloan. Sloan became a global management guru. His ideas of decentralized, multi-divisional corporations remain organizational models for today's global businesses.

The change to Sloan's "federal decentralization" marked a paradigm shift for business. Previously, decision-making was typically concentrated at head office, but a business consisting of autonomous operating divisions, subject to centralized financial and policy control, was far better suited to expand and diversify into new international markets. Sloan introduced other innovations for market growth. Under him, GM produced different makes of car to target consumers in different income brackets; not only did one product not compete with another, but owners began to aspire to "trade up" – a message Sloan reinforced with annual styling updates.

Money, politics, and power

With increasing global economic integration, a downturn in a major economy can rapidly affect other countries. The seemingly unassailable economic position of the US following the First World War was swiftly to collapse. The Great Depression that followed spread worldwide, leading to an economic global downturn, and once more to war.

A global downturn

In the late 1920s US growth went into reverse. Among the causes were over-production of goods, and deliberate inflation of money supply with offers of credit, combined with interest rates kept artificially low to support US exports. The resulting Wall Street Crash of 1929 saw millions of dollars wiped off share values. The decade-long Great Depression that followed spread outward to produce a global economic downturn.

Erecting barriers to trade

As international trade went into decline, individual nations made frantic attempts to shore up their own economies. Protectionist measures* spread, as heavy tariffs imposed on imported goods by the US led to retaliatory measures by other countries; currencies were devalued to increase the competitiveness of exports. As banks, businesses, shops, and factories closed, job losses and rising prices destabilized governments and nationalist political movements gained ground from western Europe to Latin America. Germany's Weimar Republic, already struggling to pay the reparations imposed on it after the First World War, collapsed, and political extremism in the shape of Fascism flourished, resulting eventually in the Second World War.

*Protectionist measures — *barriers to international trade erected by national governments in order to protect the interests of their domestic industries and producers.*

Recovering economies

European economies were devastated by this second global war. To aid their economic recovery and to promote political stability, security and the reestablishment of markets and international trade, US Secretary of State George C. Marshall devised the European Recovery Program or Marshall Plan of US financial aid. By 1951 industrial production in western Europe showed growth of 30 per cent compared with that at the onset of war in 1939. The role of the US in promoting European recovery reinforced its renewed standing as a global economic power – indeed *the* global economic power – until the late 20th century.

Although, as one of the Allied Powers, Russia was entitled to claim Marshall Plan aid, it refused, labelling it "dollar imperialism" – presaging the early (usually pejorative) use of the word "Americanization" to describe globalisation. Forming their own Council for Mutual Economic Assistance (Comecon), the USSR, together with other Eastern European members, withdrew behind an "iron curtain" that was to isolate them from world trade until the late 20th century.

International trade bodies

The globalising process needs a framework of international agreements and alliances, and a stable global economy, in order to develop. Both the Great Depression and the Second World War were catalysts for a new era of globally forged relationships. International trade bodies were formed to provide a structure within which individual nations could both compete and collaborate in their pursuit of domestic and global interests.

The "Bretton Woods institutions"

*The World Bank — *An internationally supported bank that provides loans to developing countries. The World Bank Group also includes three other bodies that work with governments and the private sector: the International Finance Corporation (IFC), the Multilateral Investment Guarantee Agency (MIGA), and the International Centre for Settlement of Investment Disputes (ICSID).*

In 1944, a United Nations conference of 45 governments at Bretton Woods, New Hampshire, US, resolved to create the International Monetary Fund (IMF) and task it with ensuring the stability of the international monetary and financial system. Today there are 185 member countries, paying into a fund that is disbursed in order to prevent and resolve crises, foster growth and employment, and alleviate poverty. The World Bank* was also conceived at Bretton Woods. A major focus of its work is reconstruction, whether following conflict, natural disasters, or humanitarian emergencies. Today poverty reduction is a major goal.

Although an attempt was made at Bretton Woods to formulate a charter governing trade relations at global level, it was not until 1948 that GATT, the General Agreement on Tariffs and Trade, was implemented. The idea was to provide both impetus to liberalize trade – sweeping away some of the protectionist barriers erected in the 1930s – and a forum for negotiation in cases of conflict of interest. In 1995 the World Trade Organization (WTO) was created to take over from GATT. Its overall goal remains to ensure the free flow of trade while guarding against potential negative social and economic side effects.

Promoting prosperity

Stakeholder theory — *the idea that companies should take account of the interests of all "stakeholders" – employees and local communities as well as shareholders, clients, and customers. The theory is that this motivates staff and will contribute to business success.*

During the 1970s, a group of organizations was created with a primarily economic focus. The World Economic Forum emerged from the European Management Forum (EMF), an initiative whose original idea was to explore how European management could catch up with that in the US. The forum also promoted the stakeholder theory* of management.

The EMF's remit was extended to include economic and social issues and in January 1974 political leaders were for the first time invited to meet, in Davos, Switzerland, to debate these issues. In 1976 the organization introduced membership for what it calls "the 1,000 leading companies in the world" and initiated a partnership with China. In 1979 it launched its Global Competitiveness Report, a league table of nations produced annually that ranks them by collating a number of factors, including infrastructure, education, and technological readiness. Its Networked Readiness Index is another useful yearly report. The forum's name was changed to World Economic Forum (WEF) in 1987 when it also extended its scope to provide a platform for resolving international conflicts.

IN FOCUS... THE G8

In 1975 the leaders of six nations – France, Japan, the US, Germany, the UK, and Italy – gathered near Paris to discuss global economic issues. The group was expanded to include Canada in 1976 and Russia in 1998, becoming the "Group of Eight" or G8. The summit has no fixed structure or permanent administration but operates on a rolling presidency with the ruling country setting the agenda for the summit. G8 summits are a major venue for discussion of globalisation and its challenges and management. Although a small grouping, the G8 is influential given the wealth of its member nations – they represent only 14–15 per cent of the world's population, yet account for more than 65 per cent of global economic output. This also makes G8 summits a target for protests by the anti-globalisation movement, as well as political, ethical, and environmental campaigners.

Regional trading blocs

The economic benefits conferred by international cooperation have inspired many countries to form trade alliances with their neighbours. Such regional integration highlights the paradox of globalisation. Given the domestic priorities of all countries, both "going regional" and "going global" mean being simultaneously outward-looking and self-interested. Regional grouping confers the power and influence to achieve this.

The EU – a "globalising" example

*Protectionism — *the shielding of the producers of a country from foreign competition, through measures that include tariffs (taxes on imports), restrictive quotas, tax cuts, and subsidies for domestic industry.*

One particular regional initiative, while largely protectionist, has spread far beyond its early borders both in terms of its own regional development and its global impact. Born of the European Coal and Steel Community, created in the aftermath of World War II, the European Union (EU) was created to promote "the economic and social progress of [member] countries" by the establishment of a customs union.

The creation of a single market within which existed healthy competition between member states boosted the European economy, which in turn encouraged global competition. Today the EU allows freedom of movement of people, goods, services, and capital within its boundaries. In a competitive global world, it allows European countries of all sizes to exert more influence when they speak with a single voice as members of one of the largest political and economic entities in the world.

The EU was officially established (as the EEC) by the Treaty of Rome in 1957. In 2008 there were 27 member countries.

Some two-thirds of EU citizens share a single currency, the euro, eliminating exchange expenses and risks and providing price transparency between participating member states. The acceptance and smooth introduction of the new currency in 2002 confounded sceptics and today the euro rivals the US dollar as an international currency.

MERCOSUR, South America's "common market", was founded in 1991, and groups Argentina, Brazil, Paraguay, Uruguay, and Venezuela.

NAFTA – the North American Free Trade Association – is a huge regional bloc, linking the US, Canada, and Mexico. The final provisions of its treaty were implemented in January 2008.

CARICOM is the trading group formed by the 15 countries of the Caribbean Community, created in 1973 as a common market.

Some global trade groupings

EFTA, the European Free Trade Association, was established in 1960 as an alternative to the wider-ranging EEC. Today EFTA has just four member countries: Iceland, Norway, Liechtenstein, and Switzerland.

AFTA was created by the Association of Southeast Asian Nations (ASEAN) in 1992. AFTA – the ASEAN Free Trade Area – includes Brunei, Cambodia, Indonesia, Laos, Malaysia, Myanmar, Philippines, Singapore, Thailand, and Vietnam.

A new model for business

Going global can enhance your access to innovations and management ideas from other countries. In the 1970s, the US and Europe, until then dominant in world trade, found that new technologies and production methods were allowing Japan to forge ahead in the global market.

Slimming down production

Despite strong opposition by industry in the US and Europe, the shift of power eastward was unstoppable. In industry after industry, including steel, ship-building, automobiles, and electronics, the Japanese surpassed US and European firms. Key to this success was a new business model based on "lean production" – itself ironically a development of American Taylorism – which was developed by carmaker Toyota following the Second World War, and widely adopted by Japanese industry. Japan's cost- and waste-cutting methods of production maximized efficiency, responding to the market and to customer requirements by maintaining a low inventory and topping up supplies when needed, or "just-in-time".

CASE STUDY

The shape of things to come

In 1962 Honda became the first Japanese organization to establish a factory in the European Union, or EEC as it was then called. Its Belgian Aalst plant covered 5,000m² and included facilities for assembly, welding, painting, and final inspection. Assembly of the first cars commenced in May 1963. Honda, at that time the world's leading motorcycle manufacturer and exporter, built the plant to avoid the high tariffs and import quotas imposed on importers into the European zone. The Belgian government and city of Aalst welcomed the investment. The minimum wage was lower than that of countries such as Germany, the location was good for transport, and there was an available pool of skilled labour.

Controlling quality

By the mid-1970s, Japanese manufacturing industries were also renowned for the quality of their output. The method by which this quality philosophy was put into practice also had its roots in the US, in the ideas of W. Edwards Deming. His "quality cycle" (or "Deming Cycle" as it is known in Japan) applied a four-step problem-solving formula in order to ensure quality control. The resulting dramatic gains by Japanese industry inspired home-grown concepts such as *Kaizen*, or "continuous improvement" throughout business. When the West woke up to Japan's success and the potential of the quality philosophy, it was widely adopted by companies such as Ford in the US and Jaguar Cars in the UK.

HOW TO...
APPLY THE DEMING QUALITY CYCLE

PLAN
Establish the objectives and processes necessary to deliver results in accordance with the specifications.

↓

DO
Implement the processes.

↓

CHECK
Monitor and evaluate the processes and results against objectives and specifications and report the outcome.

↓

ACT
Apply actions to the outcome for necessary improvement. This means reviewing all steps (Plan, Do, Check, Act) and modifying the process to improve it before its next implementation.

The new global players

Globalisation today has been driven by dramatic changes in the world that have freed up previously closed regions and stimulated trade and economic development. The recent dramatic economic development of China and India signals a return in terms of geography to the earliest innovators in the process of globalisation. The recovery of the Russian economy and growth in Brazil herald further shifts in economic power.

The rise of the BRICs*

BRICs — *the four largest global powers after the US and the EU, namely Brazil, Russia, India, and China. Together they account for almost 2.8 billion people, some 40 per cent of the total global population.*

Since the 1980s, the world has seen extraordinary changes. Europe's Cold War, the post-war stand-off between west and east, ended with the fall of the Berlin Wall in 1989. Since then, Russia has emerged as a major player on the global economic field, notably in the energy sector. The decline of Communism saw the opening-up and development of Eastern Europe. Countries in Eastern Europe have attracted strong inward investment while providing a substantial emigrant workforce, notably to Western Europe.

While Japan's extraordinary growth in the 1960s, '70s, and '80s turned to decline by the end of the '90s, in 1978 Communist China began the process of opening up its markets to the outside world. This has resulted in a fast-growing and hugely powerful Chinese economy with a vibrant private sector that offers unprecedented opportunities to investors.

The 1990s also saw changes made to Brazil's economic strategy. Brazilian trade and industry, previously heavily subsidized but also constrained by government intervention and regulation, were liberalized in 1990 in response to a fiscal crisis. India, too, opened up for trade in 1991 when a liberalization programme reduced trade barriers and removed investment restrictions.

Shifting power bases

India's enormous size and its capabilities in the English language – increasingly the global "language of business" – have provided extensive offshoring opportunities to the industries of the West. The service industry is particularly prominent. The IT, outsourcing, and business solutions industry in India, and notably Infosys, Tata Consultancy Services (TCS), and Wipro, now competes with major Western organizations such as Accenture and IBM.

The lure of competitively priced skills and labour have seen the most powerful of the BRICs – China and India – become offshore powerhouses for, respectively, manufacturing and services for Western business. Both now have strongly developing industries of their own with a growing global presence. And to Western companies facing mature markets at home, both China and India offer vast new marketplaces for goods and services. The rapid growth in the Indian and Chinese economies is changing the balance of world power.

CASE STUDY

A modern global giant

Established in 1945, Tata Motors, India's largest automobile company, was also the first Indian automobile company to be listed on the New York Stock Exchange. Today it has diversified into the Tata Group, and is one of India's largest business conglomerates. It has operations in more than 80 countries spanning six continents and its companies export products and services to 85 countries. Revenues in 2006–2007 reached $28.8 billion, representing some 3.2 per cent of the country's GDP.

Tata has 98 operating companies in seven business sectors ranging from information systems and communications through engineering, materials, energy, chemicals, consumer products, and services. Among its most recent acquisitions are the prestigious Jaguar and Land Rover marques from Ford Motor. Tata also now owns Corus (formerly British Steel) and Tetley, archetypal British tea merchant and inventor of the tea bag – developments with some piquancy given India's colonial past.

Chapter 2

What drives globalisation?

Key engines of change in the globalising process include economic forces, politics, power shifts, competition for resources and markets, and consumer demand – fuelled by the now-constant electronic traffic in information and knowledge.

Exchanging information

New technology and the "information revolution" have impacted not only on ease of communication but also on methods of production, distribution, marketing, and business organization. Technological change and innovation are facilitators and drivers of economic growth and globalisation.

Building the "global village"

The idea of a "global village" was introduced over 40 years ago by Canadian academic and media analyst Marshall McLuhan. At the time, some thought his ideas fanciful, but today they sound unsurprising. McLuhan was interested in how technology affected human beings and relationships between them in a society that was increasingly integrated by instant communication. He suggested that the global reach of new communications media enabled us to see the impact of our actions on a global scale, forcing us to take responsibility for them.

Working in new ways

The term "global village" today still expresses McLuhan's ideas but it also describes the practical reality of an ever-more closely linked business world. In our electronically enabled environment, you can frequently base new business links and working relationships on virtual rather than face-to-face contact.

• **Using videoconferencing** instead of physical conferencing opens up additional opportunities for international participation. Podcasts can be used to provide instantly available online briefings.
• **Using mobile phones**, SMS messaging, and handheld computers for any-time, any-place communication. In addition, VOIP broadband communication and services such as Skype have slashed call costs – an especially valuable development for small businesses; any individual with a broadband connection can confer "real-time" with contacts around the world in both sound and vision.
• **Exploring home-working, remote-working** and outsourcing possibilities. These are leading to new ways of managing workers and of assessing the value of individuals' expertise, flexibility, and performance.
• **Considering flexible working times**, which reflect the need to balance the requirements of a 24/7 world with those of the individual.
• **Using all the potential of the internet**, companies of any size can easily and instantly access sources of information, products, and services, and can market their products and services widely at low cost. Online access can also help you in the process of "buying in" outside expertise such as legal, accountancy, design, editorial, or business consultancy capabilities. Identifying and accessing such expertise is faster and easier than ever before.

Opening up markets

The past three decades have seen extraordinary changes in the world, freeing up previously closed regions and stimulating trade and economic development. The decline of Communism saw the opening-up and development of Eastern Europe and the former Soviet Union. The rapid growth in the Indian and Chinese economies is changing the balance of world power, which was previously dominated by the US.

An irreversible trend

*Export credit agencies —
institutions providing government-backed loans, guarantees, and insurance to private companies doing business overseas, thus offering them some protection from commercial and political risk in global ventures.

Open markets and free trade enable and promote global development and growth. Tariffs (taxes on imports) have long been used by governments to protect their own food producers and manufacturing industries from competitively priced imports but, since the late 1940s, international efforts have focused on dismantling these to promote a free flow of trade. At the same time, to promote exports, there exist many national and regional schemes such as export credit agencies* and the services of promotional agencies.

Politics and power

Competition between countries and companies to exploit both new and existing markets is ever fiercer – this in itself being both a result, and a driver, of globalisation. At national level, governments do all in their power to attract foreign investment. The overall result of these trends is that most of the world now forms part of a global, capitalist market economy. There have also been major new regional market developments in which the traditional groupings of wealthy countries are being challenged. A good example is the entry and increasingly powerful presence of China in valued African markets.

China in Africa

Attracted by the potential of Africa's vast natural resources, and particularly oil, to sustain China's booming economy, China has moved into a swathe of countries, offering trade deals, loans, aid packages, and improvements to infrastructure. On the one hand, this is a welcome boost to sub-Saharan economies. On the other, a flood of inexpensive Chinese-made products is hurting local producers. To Western businesses and governments, the Chinese incursion poses not only a competitive but also a political problem. China's policy is one of non-interference: it does business with some controversial African governments that the West has tried to isolate.

Erosion of statehood

The global pursuit of free-trade capitalism, surge in cross-border capital movements, and interlinking of economies have posed questions about the shrinking autonomy and leverage of individual nation states. In addition, high visibility in an electronic communications-driven world focuses NGO and media attention on national leaders. Questions arise as to why they cannot act more quickly to find global solutions to challenges such as poverty and climate change. Meanwhile a growing "club" of powerful and wealthy philanthropists, having made fortunes from global trade and finance, are taking steps independently of governments or political affiliations to target major global problems such as disease, illiteracy, and unemployment.

Gaining global momentum

The removal of trade barriers and tariffs, plus cheaper transport costs brought by technological advances in logistics and distribution, has allowed multinationals to flourish. Just as they benefit from globalisation in terms of cheaper global sourcing and huge new markets, so the competition between them further drives the globalising process.

The rise of the multinationals

The growth of modern multinational corporations can be traced back to the 19th century, which saw European colonization of many regions of the world and development of the "New World" (North and South America). This "high age of imperialism", as it is sometimes called, has been described as the first era of globalisation. US corporations subsequently dominated the 20th century. While they continue to do so into the 21st century, a new wave of multinational corporations – many based in countries currently outside the traditional economic groupings such as the WEF and G8 – is reshaping the global league tables. In 2007, the FT (*Financial Times*) annual global rankings listed the top five countries, in terms of global market value, as the US with 184 companies, Japan with 49, the UK with 41, France with 32, and Germany with 20. However, China, joining the list for the first time, went straight in at 7th place with eight large global companies, all complete newcomers. Hong Kong achieved 14th position with another eight companies.

FTSE GLOBAL 100
Lists the top 100 from the FTSE Multinationals Index (of corporations deriving more than 30 per cent of revenue outside their region) by market capitalization.

Global performance rankings of multinational corporations

FORBES 2000

Lists the world's largest public corporations using sales, profits, assets, and market value to provide a composite ranking which it considers more indicative of companies' importance to the world's economy than ranking on any single factor.

FORTUNE GLOBAL 500

Ranks the 500 largest global corporations by gross revenue (turnover). It can be searched to identify performance by country and region, climbers, losers, arrivals, and exits, and top performers by industry on a number of financial indices.

How global business connects

Exploiting the global market can involve establishing complex supply chains criss-crossing the world from raw material source to processor, manufacturer, wholesaler, retailer, and eventual customer.

The Adidas Group, for example, outsources over 95 per cent of production of its sports shoes, clothes, and accessories to third-party manufacturers, mostly in Asia. In 2007 this involved working with 377 manufacturing partners who in turn work with others such as sourcing agents and subcontractors. Adidas also has its own manufacturing sites in Germany, Sweden, Finland, the US, Canada, China, and Japan.

Further back down the supply chain, Adidas is a customer of Pittards, a British company that specializes in innovative, high-quality engineered leather products for leading brands of gloves, shoes, sports equipment, and luxury leather goods. Pittards originally had its own raw materials division in Scotland, processing Scottish sheepskins for company use and sale to third-party tanneries. In 2005 it transferred tanning operations to Ethiopia, forming a joint venture with Ethiopia Tannery Share Co., a long-standing partner in supply of glove leathers, notably sheep- and goatskins. A year later Pittards signed a licensing agreement for footwear leathers with its Taiwanese partner Teh Chang.

Pittards imports raw skins from countries such as Ethiopia, Nigeria, and the Sudan, and other raw materials and chemicals from around the world including Jordan, Yemen, Indonesia, Brazil, Peru, New Zealand, and the US. The company exports engineered leather to over 30 countries from Europe to North America, India, Pakistan, the Philippines, and the Far East. Its many major clients include Lacoste, Nike, Head, Hummel, Rawlings, SportHill, Timex, Kenzo, Footjoy, and Camper.

Exerting influence

Many questions surround the power and influence of multinationals, and the way in which the "value chain" of goods is distorted when they are sourced or produced in one country at very low cost, to become very high-value items in the countries in which they are sold – one result being that a significant number of multinational corporations have revenues exceeding the GNP of some countries. Corporations of such size and reach are not only engines of economic growth but also significant agents of sociological and political change, which poses important issues of accountability and governance.

Consuming in new ways

On the consumer side, the availability of an ever-larger and in many cases ever-cheaper range of products has driven demand in wealthier countries while growing affluence and consumer aspirations have boosted sales in developing countries. Across the world, consumers have become used to buying products and services originating in far-flung countries; foreign brands are increasingly familiar and in many cases much prized – for example, branded luxury goods and popular casual and sportswear.

The use of search engines, social and professional networking, blogging, and other forms of interaction brings unprecedented power to the individual, but also allows unprecedented access by business to information on consumer habits, trends, and desires. New technology has given birth to innovative forms of advertising, such as so-called "viral" campaigns. The electronic harvesting of consumer information based on internet browsing and purchasing history – the focus of much concern by civil liberties organizations – enables marketing to be very specifically targeted.

Barriers to globalisation

Globalisation is built on open markets but progress to a global market economy is not always smooth. National governments are expected to protect and develop their economies and this involves controls. Despite international efforts to liberalize markets, protectionist measures in the form of import taxes and other non-tariff barriers* persist today.

Liberalizing trade

*Non-tariff barrier — *while a tariff is another word for a tax, a non-tariff barrier to trade, or NTB, can take many forms. These may include subsidies to domestic producers, import quotas and licences, special packaging and labelling regulations, and health and safety rules.*

While huge changes have taken place, the tendency for nation states to seek advantage for or protect their own economies and interests is strong. Efforts to liberalize trade by the World Trade Organization (WTO) involve multilateral agreements – agreements between several countries. Membership of the WTO should entail extending "most favoured nation" status – that is, equal trading opportunities – to all other members. But many governments still resort to unilateral policies (policies pursued by one country in isolation) – especially to protect the livelihoods of individuals in politically influential domestic industries.

Guarding traditional industries

Unilateral trade policies are common in agriculture, both to protect food supplies and preserve traditional "cultural ways of life". In some countries particularly strong protection is given to staple product industries – that is, crops or other products with a long history of production in that country, such as rice in Japan, or wine in France – especially where those industries face competition from low-cost producers elsewhere in the world. At one point, Japan's tariffs on imported rice would have made it 1,000 per cent more expensive for the consumer than Japanese-grown rice.

Examples of protectionist measures

IMPORT QUOTAS

Governments can impose two types of import quota: tariff quotas that restrict the total volume or value of goods imported at preferential tariffs; and quantity quotas that limit imports overall.

ANTI-DUMPING MEASURES

Taken to combat proven cases of "dumping" – when goods are exported for sale at less than the price charged for them in the exporter's home market.

RULES OF ORIGIN

Used to determine the country or region of origin of goods, either where they have been wholly obtained or produced, or where the last significant process in manufacture took place. They determine if imported goods are subject to quotas or attract preferential rates of duty.

LOCAL CONTENT REQUIREMENTS (LCR)

Governments impose these to regulate foreign direct investment and promote local manufacturing capacity and employment over imports. LCR also favours technology transfer because the foreign company will need to work closely with suppliers of locally made components to ensure compatibility and quality.

DOCUMENTATION REQUIREMENTS

Using "red tape" to deter imports by requiring huge amounts of accompanying documentation: certificates, declarations, licences, waybills, and bank instructions.

CASE STUDY

The rise of cheap clothing

In 2005 the decades-old international framework for trade in clothing and textiles – the Multi-Fibre Arrangement – was abolished. This meant that there would no longer be import quotas imposed on these goods. The result was that cheaper products from Asia, and especially China, flooded Western markets, welcomed by retailers and consumers. This resulted in a huge and rapid shift in production away from western Europe, Japan, and the US, towards Asia (particularly China), Mexico, and Eastern Europe. China's 4 per cent share of the world market in 1985, for example, rose to some 25 per cent. Both the US and the EU tried to stall the process of dismantling the MFA in order to protect their own textile industries. When this failed, they promptly imposed import quotas on Chinese garments. But as soon as the quotas were announced, retailers and wholesalers rushed to order supplies from China, using up the limits almost as soon as they were introduced – a prime example of the conflicts a liberalized market can create between the needs of domestic producers and consumers.

Measures imposed by wealthy countries to protect their domestic industries are hugely controversial. It would seem reasonable for producers in country A to want to defend their livelihoods against a tide of low-priced imports from country B, where cheap labour and materials costs may give producers a massive competitive advantage. But consumers in country A may well prefer to have the option of buying cheap products from country B. Wealthy countries may also use their resources to subsidize domestic industries, depressing world prices at the expense of producers in underdeveloped countries. The US, for example, has been widely criticized for subsidizing its maize farmers heavily, then selling the corn very cheaply to Mexico, damaging the livelihoods of Mexican maize farmers.

Arbitrating on disputes

*Common External Tariff — *import tax imposed equally by all members of a customs union on all goods entering the area from any country outside the group.*

Regional trading bloc policies favouring member countries over non-members can also act as barriers to global fair trade. Attempts by the EU, for example, to protect its member states' interests have targeted both clothing imports and cars, with the imposition of a Common External Tariff* on imports. All EU member states benefit from this trade protection.

Countries disputing both unilateral and regional protectionist actions may appeal to the World Trade Organization, and WTO rulings often reveal how protectionist measures distort trade. The longest-running dispute in WTO history is the so-called "banana trade war", in which a WTO panel recently found that the EU banana import regime flouted global trade rules. Because of historic links relating to member states' colonial histories, the EU has long given preferential access to bananas from specific African, Caribbean, and Pacific (ACP) countries, in the process discriminating against those from elsewhere, notably Latin America. In 2001 the EU agreed to adopt a tariff-only regime that would ensure total market access by January 1 2006. However, it failed to keep to this commitment, instead introducing a 750,000 tonne zero-duty tariff quota for bananas from ACP countries but a €176 ($260) per tonne tariff on bananas from other countries. Critics of the WTO argue that it has neither the teeth nor the inclination to ensure wealthy Western nations play by its rules.

Anti-globalisation

Globalisation became a media phenomenon when it reached beyond the worlds of business and finance and into wide public consciousness – paradoxically, through the mass anti-globalisation protests in Seattle in 1999 and at subsequent G8 summits. The protesters came from all over the world and represented many different interests. Some were environmentalists, others anti-capitalist or humanitarian.

Levelling criticism

The common theme of the "anti" movement is discontent at the human and environmental costs of globalisation, and the fact that the benefits are very unevenly shared. Global integration, they claim, is in effect a power struggle among the wealthy, rather than an attempt to "level the playing field" of the world. Some specific criticisms are hard to refute, as they encompass what could be called defining characteristics or "byproducts" of market capitalism:

• The progressive reduction of trade and investment barriers leads to downward pressure on wages;

• The accelerating pace of technological change leads to greater job insecurity and the end of the lifetime employment system;

• Inadequate environmental standards in some host countries leads to increases in pollution – a so-called "unpriced externality"* of global businesses;

• Greater income inequality emerges, both within countries and between them, creating new sociological and political divisions;

• The power of the state is eroded;

• Deregulation of industry and services leads to greater opportunities for stock-market speculation.

*Unpriced externalities — *costs, such as pollution and an increase in landfill, on the local environment and economy of host countries caused by the activities of foreign business located there.*

A new imperialism

In addition to warnings of the economic exploitation of poorer countries, there are fears of another less tangible, but no less emotive, development. Opponents of globalisation argue that the exposure of consumers in newly opened markets to the goods, brands, and services of the developed world will result in a steady homogenization of consumer tastes and aspirations – and hence the erosion of cultural diversity. Some "Old World" European countries with a strong sense of national identity also see globalisation as eroding their culture and imposing an Anglo-Saxon, particularly American, way of life characterized by increasing numbers of low-paid and part-time jobs with little or no security. Whether the impact is economic, social, or cultural, the perception that globalisation is driven by particular vested interests and cultures also encourages perceptions and fears of a new "cultural imperialism". This can lead to a rise in nationalist tendencies. The many challenges of globalisation are made ever more pressing by the rapid pace of change and the absence of effective governance including a global code of ethics.

Bio-piracy – the "hijacking" of indigenous resources

"Bio-piracy" is the negative term for Western attempts to exploit and patent local knowledge and resources in the developing world. Both the EU and US, for example, granted multiple patents on the oil from India's neem tree, long recognized in India for its beneficial properties. The US also tried to grant patents on turmeric – long used in South Asia for its healing properties – and even basmati rice. These last two attempts were successfully, and very expensively, fought off, but it is rare for poor countries to have the resources to defend themselves against such actions.

Chapter 3

Doing business in a global world

There are many routes to global expansion, from outsourcing one component of your business to major offshore investment. Careful planning and above all research are essential to both your globalising strategy and your sales in new markets.

Deciding to "go global"

Many developed Western markets are showing low or no growth, yet are increasingly competitive. As a strategy, "going global" offers extensive marketing possibilities in addition to potential savings in operating costs. These cost savings favour competitive pricing, enhancing marketing potential and boosting growth and overall competitiveness.

Planning your global future

*Outsourcing and offshoring — "outsourcing" simply means contracting one aspect of your company's business to another company, which may be in the same country. Outsourcing abroad is "offshoring".

The aim in considering a global strategy will generally be to optimize your global value chain – that is, maximize revenue but with an outlay that guarantees the quality of your product or service – through such options as global sourcing, franchising, outsourcing and offshoring* or FDI (foreign direct investment), location of factories, and distribution channels. A large company may have the skills it needs in-house to plan for expansion, but if yours is a small company, you may need to buy in advice and expertise.

Gaining from globalisation

*USP — *Unique Selling Point – what it is that makes your products or services special or different from those of your competitors.*

Your organization's global potential will depend on its size and location, market, resources, innovation, and aspirations. You will need to know where it stands, i.e. the marketing potential based on its USP*, and what strengths, weaknesses, opportunities, and threats would emerge in pursuing your objectives.

Consider the range of opportunities offered by global expansion, and which ones are a fit for you:
• New business growth in wider/new markets
• Benefiting from access to natural resources – raw materials, skilled labour, local talent pools/expertise
• Reducing competition by acquiring competitors
• Global marketing and branding
• Finding new markets for older products, and developing new products more suited to non-domestic markets
• Use of a foreign location as a regional "hub", giving you easier access to a cluster of markets
• Economies of scale: ability to buy raw materials at lower cost; ability to produce more at lower cost
• Lower cost production or services, e.g. cheaper labour, higher productivity
• 24/7 operating, for example offering continuous call-centre service across time zones
• Financial benefits, e.g. subsidies, favourable exchange or interest rates, fewer or lower taxes
• Easier/cheaper operating environments – less bureaucracy, less legislation, avoidance of tariffs or trade barriers through foreign direct investment (FDI).

ASK YOURSELF...
WHAT'S OUR GAME PLAN?

• What are we looking for?
 – cost reductions?
 – growth?
 – new markets?
 – new product potential?
 – first-mover potential?
 – second-mover potential?
• Need we go global?
• What will it cost?
• Can we afford it?
• What skills will we need?
• Should we outsource/offshore?
• Should we offer franchises?
• How do we find/select suppliers?
• Should we consider a merger, acquisition, or FDI?
• What are the management implications?
• What are the risks?

Extending your range

There are many ways to spread your business across borders, from locating your own production facilities abroad to offering your products or services in a virtual international market via the Internet. Inevitably, strategies range from the extremely complex, especially where you are committing to foreign direct investment, to the relatively straightforward – provided that you have fully explored the key issues and risks involved.

Expanding abroad

*****Organic growth** — *increasing the turnover of an existing business by introducing new products, growing sales via new outlets, or building factories to increase production and sales.*

To compete globally, businesses can expand through:
• Greenfield investment – setting up sales outlets or manufacturing facilities abroad (organic growth*)
• Mergers and acquisitions
• Strategic alliances
• Exports
• A distribution deal or franchising operation
• An internet trading operation capable of handling international transactions and delivery.

Defining your aims

The complexity of your expansion strategy will vary according to the country of origin of your business, your target market, the nature of your product or service, and the type of global operation you envisage. For example, a company planning to establish a new sales outlet or to build a factory will need not only to work with the local or regional authorities to obtain planning permission, but also with lawyers and accountants to ensure local laws are respected. The alternative is to acquire or merge with an established local firm. While this reduces the risks and uncertainties of a start-up in unfamiliar surroundings, thorough due diligence* is essential.

Doing your homework

Whichever route to expansion you choose, your research will need to focus on a range of issues. All businesses need to research market potential and conditions, risks, and challenges. An export business or franchiser may later have to deal with sales agents or individual businesses abroad, together with supplementary paperwork including contracts, invoices, shipping documentation, correspondence, accounting, and tax matters.

***Due diligence** — *the in-depth investigation of all aspects of a business prior to merger or acquisition.*

Operating a business in more than one country

To set up and run a subsidiary company abroad, or to locate a division of your firm in another country, will involve a substantial commitment of resources and a major strategic challenge. You must evaluate what in your existing company model and policies will translate across borders.

Designing new systems

Establishing a new business abroad will mean putting a management system in place; it may mirror that of corporate headquarters or it may need to be adapted to suit local conditions. Management issues include:

- **Strategies** relating to investment, R&D and innovation, markets, sourcing, production, sales, packaging, and marketing;
- **Policies** relating to employment and remuneration, training, and equal opportunities;
- **Corporate culture and practices** relating to communications, sustainability*, and ethics.

*Sustainability —
your firm's "green"
credentials and
ethical policies
regarding such
issues as energy use,
responsible sourcing
of materials, working
conditions, training,
and job security.*

Structuring options

Management of your multinational business may be centralized, with head office taking all decisions. It may be devolved, with subsidiaries that are entirely independent, or partially devolved, with the head office ruling solely on certain issues, typically strategy and finance but possibly also product and concept development. How much duplication of function this entails depends on what structure, or operating model, your global venture adopts.

Vertical operating model

If you are marketing a product whose core values are authenticity and a strong commitment to sustainable manufacture, you may choose to have a vertically structured business. Your global growth and development will run backwards along the "supply chain" to the production of raw materials, giving you more control over sourcing and manufacture than is achieved by subcontracting to third parties. ECCO, the Danish family-run footwear manufacturer, is just such a firm, claiming to be the only manufacturer in the world to control "the entire value chain from cow to shoe". It has its own tanneries, five ECCO factories located across the world, and five ECCO sales hubs in three continents.

Horizontal operating model

Horizontal operating, at its simplest, means "doing the same thing in multiple locations", and who your competitors are in each market will be critical to success. It includes selling global products such as Apple® or Coca-Cola®; offering professional services worldwide; as Ernst & Young does; or exporting a retailing concept, such as the Swedish furnishing giant IKEA. Horizontal operators may also extend vertical supply chains downward, either centrally or in multiple locations, or contract out their manufacturing: UK retailer Tesco, for example, has multiple sources for goods worldwide. Horizontal operating thus focuses on a "core function", whereas vertical operating requires commitment to many stages in production.

Going "glocal"

A multinational operating model for a business that recognizes cultural and geographical differences and adapts its expansion strategies, operating structures, practices, products, and services to local markets is called "glocal". This global/local model gave rise to the mantra "think globally – act locally" that was so popular in the 1990s.

TIP

GET YOUR EAR TO THE GROUND

Many countries subsidize business fact-finding trips to foreign markets. Check with your country's export promotion bureau.

Thinking laterally

To build a glocal model, you need to re-evaluate the core values and image of your product or service from a global perspective. Which of your messages will work well outside your home market? Could they be tailored to work better? Could the product or service be adapted? Or would it be better to join forces with a local firm?

For glocalizing inspiration, look to French firm Danone, best known in Europe for dairy products, which has fully exploited a glocal strategy, using investment, acquisitions, and alliances to create a global portfolio of products with specific appeal to local markets. In China, where adult consumption of dairy products is low, it has a share in Chinese fruit juice producer Hui Yuan, but has also created a niche market for a hawthorn-flavoured yoghurt. In Russia, it produces a probiotic version of the traditional fermented milk and grain drink, kefir. In Latin America and Eastern Europe, it has tapped into huge new demand for flavoured waters. In Indonesia, sales of its bottled water fund a local initiative to improve access to clean water. Marketing is tailored to the health and social preoccupations of the culture; yoghurt is "healthful for children" in China and Spain, but "promotes regularity" in the constipated US. In France, Danone even launched a "beauty yoghurt" said to enhance the complexion.

Spreading risk

Although it does require significant investment in market and product research, the glocal strategy of a mixed product portfolio spread widely across markets can give you several advantages. Acquiring or forming alliances with local firms with a proven track record saves considerably on costs compared with FDI. If you have international partners well acquainted with local markets, your company will be well positioned to spot and exploit new high-growth areas. Local recessions can also more easily be weathered. As Danone CEO Franck Riboud said in 2006: "Our growth is not dependent on ups and downs in any part of the world... With our broad geographical base, we can make up for the temporary lulls that are inevitable in any market."

ASK YOURSELF...
COULD WE GO GLOCAL?

- Can my firm's capabilities and products be reconfigured to appeal to different markets?
- Which new growth areas in our sector are currently under-represented in the target market?
- Which predicted growth areas in our home market could be expected to spread into foreign markets?
- What niche in our industry is least well served in the target market?
- Which local firms offer a product or service that would dovetail with the portfolio and business strengths of our existing set-up?
- Have we fully investigated the circumstances of local firms bidding for a global partner?
- Have they previously been involved in a joint venture? If it failed, why?

CASE STUDY

A global giant goes glocal

Wal-Mart started life as a single discount store in 1962 in Rogers, Arkansas, US. Today it is a global giant, channelling its highly structured retail concept via, in 2008, some 3,000 stores outside the US. Yet even Wal-Mart had to "glocalize" its product range and operating model when it ventured into China. The company has a centralized, global buying agency for the products it sells, but in China, it had to adapt. The high demand for fresh produce, particularly leafy green vegetables, meant that supplies had to be sourced locally and store design reconfigured with larger produce aisles. Chinese government regulations required the firm to source alcoholic drinks and tobacco products locally. Add to this the loyalty of Chinese consumers to Chinese brands, and it is hardly surprising that 85 per cent of products sold in Chinese Wal-Mart stores come from Chinese suppliers.

Outsourcing and offshoring

Outsourcing and offshoring add a new dimension to the concept of "sourcing". While countries across the world have for centuries been tapped for their natural resources, their use as a large-scale source of processed or semi-processed products, labour, skills, and expertise has vastly increased with globalisation.

Operating in cost-driven markets

High costs in some countries and the need to compete with lower-cost businesses have resulted in companies relocating production within their own countries or, alternatively, outsourcing manufacturing and service operations to other countries – in other words, "offshoring". The US footwear company Nike, for example, is a direct or indirect employer of almost one million people. It operates in more than 160 countries and subcontracts production to manufacturers worldwide, notably in China and Southeast Asia.

Choosing a destination

Finding an offshore partner depends to a large degree on which aspect of your business you are looking to outsource – manufacturing and assembly, in which case transport costs must be factored in, or business process operations, whether customer-facing or back-office functions such as accountancy and data processing. India is currently the top choice as the major offshore supplier of IT and call centre services. India's IT industry enjoyed a massive boost in commissions from the West during the preparations for Y2K* when, with its ample workforce and expertise, it was able to focus on the issue in a way that the US and other Western nations lacked the resources to do.

*Y2K preparations — *measures taken to safeguard global computer systems in anticipation of problems (which in fact did not materialize) caused by the date rolling over from 1999 to 2000 – widely referred to as the "millennium bug".*

ADVANTAGES OF OFFSHORING

Cost reductions

Access to fresh talent pool

Flexibility: e.g. achieving 24/7 service by spreading call centres across time zones

Access to latest technologies without upgrading at home

Access when needed to high-quality services (e.g. IT) rather than maintaining in-house expertise

PLACING WORK ABROAD

DISADVANTAGES OF OFFSHORING

Risk of quality and management problems

Damage to image if offshore management treats workers badly

Risk of loss of control/security issues e.g. theft of intellectual property

Possible customer resistance

Damage to image in home country if domestic jobs are lost

CASE STUDY

"Rightshoring" – a new global delivery model

In what could be described as a "reverse" offshoring strategy, Firstsource (previously ICICI OneSource), India's fifth-largest business process management services provider and a leading global provider, now has call centre operations in the UK, US, Argentina, and the Philippines, serving companies that do not wish to offshore to India. Founded in 2001 and ranked third in a *BusinessWeek* list of "hot players" in the offshore outsourcing world, Firstsource's "rightshoring" model blends onshore and offshore delivery capabilities through 33 delivery centres across four continents. It offers proximity to clients and access to a global talent pool. Its global delivery model includes 17,000 employees in Indian and other centres. Firstsource's services cover customer acquisition and care, transaction processing, billing, and collections. The organization has over 70 global clients including several Fortune 500 and FTSE 100 companies.

Considering the case against

If you are seeking to offshore, you need to bear in mind that it remains an emotive subject, given the domestic job losses, both actual and perceived, it can entail. A famous example occurred in 2003, when the US State of Indiana put out a tender to upgrade the computer system that processed the state's unemployment claims. Tata America Ltd, the US-based arm of India's Tata Consultancy Services, easily won the contract, undercutting bids from US firms such as Deloitte and Accenture by almost a third. Thus employment was created in India at the expense of jobs in Indiana – ironically, in the very state department dealing with joblessness. The move caused a political storm. If you are in a sector where local employment issues are sensitive, carefully weigh the cost advantages of offshoring against the risk of damage to your image – or consider the "rightshoring" or "nearshoring" options offered by firms such as Firstsource (*see above*).

Levelling the field

Today, firms are able to slice their activities ever more finely, separating off and relocating each in the most cost-effective location. *New York Times* columnist Thomas L. Friedman, in his book *The World is Flat*, sees this as a process that will gradually level the global playing field, empowering emergent nations as they seize the opportunities on offer. Friedman took his inspiration from the Indian firms Wipro and Infosys, avowed "flat world" companies who built on outsourced business to become global giants in their own right.

As production is offshored from developed to less-developed nations, so valuable knowledge, investment, and technology is also transferred. Taiwan, for example, used to be the number one offshore destination for the manufacture of semiconductors – for example, computer memory chips – but today is a world leader in their design. As expertise spreads, salaries will undoubtedly rise in countries such as India and Taiwan, resulting in them losing their competitive edge – but by then, some say it will be too late to bring the work back to the West.

? ASK YOURSELF...

SHOULD WE OFFSHORE?

- Have we obtained tenders from local as well as offshore firms?
- Will our decision be based on cost alone?
- Will our management strategies and policies work across borders?
- How will communication/ knowledge transfer be effected – and protected?
- Is data security an issue?
- Will our offshore activities have a negative environmental impact? How can we offset this?
- Can the outsourcer demonstrate a good record with regard to employment conditions?

The theory is that, as workers in the developed world lose out to those in emergent nations, particularly in what are called the STEM fields – science, technology, engineering, and mathematics – then students in higher education in those developed nations would have no incentive to train in these subjects. The West as a whole would eventually lose its expertise in these and other areas, and thus become dependent on the erstwhile offshore providers.

Seizing opportunities for small businesses

There has never been a better time for small and medium-sized firms to target foreign markets. They even have an advantage in that their small size makes them more able to change, innovate, and adapt quickly to meet changing market needs – crucial in a fast-moving competitive world.

TIP

USE OFFSHORE FREELANCERS
Language permitting, new technology makes it perfectly possible to use freelancers in other countries for many jobs. Outsourcing small, unrelated tasks to freelancers is popularly known as "bodyshopping".

Operating as a micro-multinational

Small companies branching out beyond their home markets have been dubbed "micro-multinationals". Their innovative profiles and success bear out theories of the benefits of smallness. They are mostly based in the US and Europe but globalisation is encouraging worldwide initiatives. Online operations can minimize office costs for small firms. A business can be run from a home office and colleagues can work together virtually, with functions such as accounting and copywriting subcontracted to freelancers if necessary. An internet search reveals any number of small businesses that operate such models.

✔ CHECKLIST SMALL FIRMS IN A GLOBAL MARKET – CRUCIAL PREPARATIONS

	YES	NO
• Do your market research	☐	☐
• Speak to business advisers	☐	☐
• Take legal advice	☐	☐
• Consult your bank and accountants	☐	☐
• Visit target markets and identify local advisers	☐	☐
• Build up relationships of trust	☐	☐
• Keep written records of discussions and, to avoid misunderstandings, send email confirmation of agreed plans of action, requesting replies	☐	☐

The case of Cobra

Some businesses have a remarkable ability to adapt to economic and market changes and trends. An example is the Cobra beer business – set up in 1989, just when a recession was biting. With a bank loan of £30,000, 27-year-old Karan Faridoon Bilimoria – a chartered accountant and graduate of Osmania University, Hyderabad, and the University of Cambridge – launched Cobra from his London flat. His aim was to market a less gassy beer to accompany the curries that are so popular in the UK. He arranged brewing in Bangalore, taking his first delivery in 1990, and cold-called Indian restaurants, making deliveries from his battered old Citroën 2CV, parked discreetly out of sight.

The business eventually took off and in 1997 production was moved from Bangalore to the UK to facilitate management. In 2004 a partnership was agreed with the largest independent brewing company in India, Mount Shivalik, to brew Cobra beer under licence for the fast-growing Indian domestic market. In early 2008 Cobra acquired its own brewery through acquisition of a controlling stake in Iceberg Industries in the state of Bihar. It also manufactures under licence in five further locations in India.

Having offshored, outsourced, and finally invested in its own manufacturing plant as part of its global development strategy, by 2008 Cobra was growing at a rate of 35 per cent per annum with some £55m in annual sales, had subsidiaries in South Africa and the US as well as India, and was selling into markets in almost 50 countries worldwide.

TIP

USE VOIP

Using Voice Over Internet Protocol (VOIP) services such as Skype will allow you to make telephone calls both over the internet and to anyone with a regular phone line. VOIP services have slashed call costs. Calls abroad cost a fraction of those in the past – a huge asset for a small company targeting global markets.

Expanding into a virtual world

While large companies are more likely to have the financial and other means to create a physical transnational presence, the growth of internet technology means that the smallest companies can research, market, and advertise a presence, sell a product, or recruit across borders as easily as, if not more so than, the big players. They can become what have been described as "engines for innovation", often by "clicks" (the internet) alone.

Thousands of small "virtual" companies are selling a raft of products and services ranging from food products to clothes, and services such as web design, software development, office services and, in wealthier markets, lifestyle management and concierge services. Some subsequently expand to become huge organizations. The online auctioneer eBay and Amazon, the online bookshop, were international from the outset, collaborating with or hiring employees in different countries, and sourcing and marketing internationally.

CASE STUDY

Virtual versus franchising

In 1999, Vietnamese–American entrepreneur Jacquelyn Tran started to develop her parents' small perfume business, taking it from a single retail outlet – that had developed from a flea-market stall – to a $20-million online fragrance, cosmetics, and hair- and skin-care sales operation. Beauty Encounter now has more than 1,000 brands and 15 per cent of sales come from abroad, notably the UK, Canada, France, Germany, Latin America, and Japan. By contrast, Anita Roddick chose the franchising route. She founded her first Body Shop outlet on the UK's south coast in 1976. By 1978 The Body Shop had its first overseas franchise – a kiosk in Brussels. By 1982 it was opening two shops a month. By 1990 it was trading in 39 countries, and by 2005 it had a total of 2,045 stores around the globe. In 2006 it was acquired by L'Oréal, which operates its 2,100 stores in 55 countries. Such cherry-picking of "green" companies by corporate giants to boost their sustainable or ethical profile is increasingly common.

TIP

WATCH THE EXCHANGE RATE

Currency and exchange rate fluctuations can sometimes work to the benefit of exporters. For example, a weak dollar boosts US exports. Conversely, a strong euro makes European imports less attractive to the US.

Creating a franchise network

If your start-up is too small to go it alone, franchising can offer another way of expanding overseas. Franchising means authorizing others to sell your goods or services on your behalf, under your organization's banner, and in a particular way specified by you. The franchising agreement you set up can specify the methods of operation by which each franchise must be run, including specific details such as the signage to be used, for example, or the decor of a retail outlet. One advantage of taking the franchise approach is that you will be able to benefit from the specific knowledge "on the ground" of the franchisees in each of the countries you want to move in to. It also means that the risk is shared with the franchisee who takes on the marketing.

The US sandwich retailer Subway® is a prime example of how a small business can rapidly expand internationally through franchising. The first franchised Subway® restaurant opened in Connecticut in 1974, and today the business has almost 30,000 franchised restaurants in 86 countries around the world.

Marketing globally

Marketing and selling globally might seem like an enticing prospect, offering economies of scale, a buffer against individual market fluctuations, and at best the opportunity to use the same marketing messages worldwide, but the reality is complex. Global markets can differ wildly in terms of size, access, ease and means of operating, and consumer values, tastes, and consumption patterns.

Getting close to target markets

A global enterprise by definition sells to markets across the world, which means its sales division will need to be close to target markets, either physically or virtually. At product level, local differences may involve tailoring marketing, packaging, brand names, or even actual products to local tastes or requirements – this is called "localization".

IN FOCUS...
ENTERING NEW MARKETS

Chocolate is still novel in China and India – consumption is measured in grammes or ounces per capita in comparison to the annual 11kg (24lbs) consumed by the British and Swiss. These new markets offer huge potential but also pose challenges. In China, Swiss Nestlé is taking market share from established market leader Mars of the US. Nestlé's Kit Kat is very popular in China, while Mars' Dove bar is considered by many too sweet. Nestlé, with its strong associations with dairy products and infant formula, may also be benefiting from the Chinese government's promotion of milk – not a traditional food in China – as nourishing for children. Other players in China include Italian Ferrero, whose Kinder and Rocher brands are proving extremely popular, but they have also been copied. Ferrero successfully sued Montresor, a Chinese company, for making fake Ferrero Rochers. Meanwhile US newcomer Hershey is adapting to local tastes by linking up with a Chinese partner; it has also introduced a green-tea-flavoured chocolate to appeal to local tastes.

Marketing online

A website is not only a virtual brochure, but a very economical way to advertise. Even the smallest company can have a professional-looking website – although surprisingly many still don't.
A website is a showcase for your products and services that can put you on a level footing with your biggest competitors globally. If you're a niche producer or service provider, your very "smallness" can make you very special.

Quality and easy access are, of course, crucial in making sure that your website gets your message across to the widest-possible audience. It has been estimated that internet users only spend an average of 44 seconds on a webpage – which means its message must be crystal clear and immediately understood by a wide range of site visitors with different linguistic and cultural profiles.

Bear in mind also that while in some countries e-commerce (trading via the internet) and such advanced logistics as electronic data interchange (EDI) and barcodes may be the norm, in others they are not. Beyond the so-called "4 Ps of Marketing" – product, price, place (distribution), and promotion – you need to take all these differences into account. As always, do your research.

ASK YOURSELF...
HOW GOOD IS YOUR WEBSITE?

- How will internet searchers find it?
- Does it have a clever name that says it all?
- Does it have links from other sites?
- Is it well designed and easily and rapidly navigable?
- Is it attractive and interesting?
- Does it immediately convey your unique selling point (USP)?
- Is the copy clear, concise, and well written?
- Does the copy have an "international" tone?
- Does it encourage visitors to browse the site further?

The golden rules

The three key stages in planning for successful sales are:
- Acquisition of reliable market intelligence;
- Dissemination of market intelligence within the company departments;
- Responsiveness to this information.

In other words, you must not only do your homework (or have it done for you), but also ensure that it is made to work for you. Open, two-way (or even multi-way) lines of communication throughout your organization are essential.

Globalising a brand

The decision to take a brand global is driven by strategic opportunities, for example being able to tap into bigger markets, achieve economies of scale, displace competitors, and drive innovation. Going global is highly attractive, but you must meet a challenging set of obligations.

Crossing cultural divides

A brand creates associations between a product or service and the qualities or characteristics that make it special or unique. Successful brands are those that understand what makes people tick and communicate this to their markets. A global brand needs to achieve this across cultural divides. Although your global brand may need to have elements of regional customization, just as the product or products may need localization, all your local variants should share common values. Your brand is one of your most valuable assets and needs particular attention if you are going to launch any products or services globally.

ASK YOURSELF... DOES MY BRAND HAVE GLOBAL POTENTIAL?

All successful brands share common features. Ask yourself whether the answer to all of these questions is "Yes":
- Is your brand highly recognizable among consumers?
- Does your brand deliver a consistent message?
- Does your brand compete along emotional lines?
- Does your brand express something unique?
- Is your brand adaptable to regional cultures, tastes, and demands?
- Do all your senior managers champion the brand?

Localizing messages

The successful global brands are those that are able to bridge the sometimes seemingly contradictory concepts of "global" and "local". To achieve this you need a strong, globally appealing message, such as "quality" or "good value", and then to be able to tailor that message to different audiences in locally relevant ways. This type of brand localization requires that regional managers have the freedom to interpret and express their own message, while still complementing the global brand. According to the 70/30 principle, it is recommended that 70 per cent of your brand should remain constant, with 30 per cent able to adapt to regional circumstances.

CASE STUDY

"Glocal" branding

Fast-food retailer McDonald's is one of the world's best known brands and the world's leading food service retailer with a presence in over 100 countries. The McDonald's model is all about standardization and American-style eating and service, but it is also a case study in localization. While hamburger and chips are a staple offering, seen by many as icons of American fast-food, the menu includes various other items, including sandwiches, wraps, and vegetarian options. Local adaptations are made to meet differing expectations around the world – a policy that, for example, has included the use of halal beef, and the introduction of localized dishes such as Bubur Ayam McD™ – a type of chicken porridge – in markets such as Malaysia, and the McBurrito™ in Mexico.

Guarding your brand

A brand is only as good as the intellectual property protection it has. If you want to be competitive and maintain your image, you must adopt an international intellectual property (IP) strategy. Trademark rights are territorial, so protection in your home country will not extend to other parts of the world. The Madrid System (administered by the World Intellectual Property Organization) allows you to file a single trademark application and then extend the protection to a large number of countries. Remember, there is no such thing as "worldwide" trademark registration: under the international Madrid System, you "pick and pay" accordingly. In other words, select the countries of commercial interest to you and pay only for those countries' filing fees. IP law has a unique requirement that you must be seen to police and enforce your trademark. Therefore you must actively fend off any infringers to preserve your mark's exclusivity.

TIP

Avoiding cross-cultural blunders

DO YOUR MARKET RESEARCH

Before launching a product in a new market, thoroughly research that country's cultural sensitivities, local tastes, and laws.

"Brand blunders" when brand names travel abroad can have disastrous results, risking being politically or culturally insensitive or sometimes hilarious. In all cases, however, it makes brand-owners look silly at best and as branding is all about image, this is damaging. The Absolut vodka company, for example, came to regret an advertising campaign that showed the southwestern part of the US as forming part of Mexico, as it had done in the 1830s, before the 1848 Mexican–American War. The ad was designed to please the Mexican market, but offended some Americans who called for a boycott. In the UK, clothing retailer Topshop had to withdraw from its stores an entire stock of t-shirts that were adorned with an attractive-looking pattern in Cyrillic script, because the text turned out to be a far-right nationalist message. Translation into other languages can be a particularly tricky area for the global brand owner. Motorola's "Hellomoto" ring tone, for example, sounds like "Hello fatty" in India; Microsoft's "Vista" means "a frumpy old woman" in Latvian; and a direct translation into Mandarin of "You're in the Pepsi Generation" rendered it as "Pepsi brings your ancestors back from the dead".

 IN FOCUS... REFRESHING A BRAND

Luxury brands are particularly vulnerable to economic downturns and changes in fashion, but can be reinvigorated in new markets. For example, a decline in the European market for cognac – the brandy produced uniquely in the Cognac region of western France – has been completely reversed over the last decade by popularity further afield.

Long a status symbol in China, cognac in recent years has seen huge demand from the Chinese middle classes. Its recovery also owes much to its clever repositioning as a fashionable long cocktail drink with mixers, rather than as the traditional after-dinner digestif popular with a more mature, and predominantly male, market.

Launching a global brand

Ensure that your brand communicates the same core meaning across every territory you intend to move into.

Undertake thorough research of your target markets in each territory, and make any adjustments to your brand that will help to give it a local competitive advantage.

Select the most appropriate communication channels to maximize the impact of your product, while minimizing the cost of advertising.

Be realistic about the significant amount of time and money it will take for markets to gradually familiarize themselves with your brand.

Invest in internal brand alignment so that all your staff are familiar with your core brand values and are able to communicate them consistently to their regional markets.

Pilot your products and packaging in each territory, to gauge reaction and highlight problematic cultural differences.

Chapter 4

Managing at a global level

Globalisation and especially global management education, notably the MBA, have made differences in nationality and business practices less evident than in the past, but managing any operation outside your base nation still poses challenges.

Setting up a team

Hiring abroad is not required for all forms of global expansion, but if you are looking to recruit in another country, then your choice of candidates, especially for teamleading or senior reporting roles, is crucial. Do your homework to ensure that you attract and secure the best people.

TIP

LOOK FOR RETURNEES

Local managers who have spent some time in your country of origin can be a real find. Check out your local university's department of management studies for overseas students from your target region.

Benefiting from local talent

Your first question will be: where are we going to recruit? It used to be common for multinationals to keep a home bias, recruiting and promoting their own nationals to local management positions. However, current thinking favours local recruitment, which has many advantages. Local managers will be more attuned to and knowledgeable about local markets, and may be able to smooth out cultural differences in management styles. Demonstrating your faith in and respect for local talent will greatly assist with your acceptance into the wider community and bring you useful contacts.

TIP

RECRUITING CHINESE GRADUATES

Chinese graduates will expect to be offered a salary that corresponds to their university's "ranking" on an unofficial but widely respected hierarchy; you should make yourself familiar with it.

Knowing local practices

To recruit abroad you need to be aware not only of legal requirements in your host country, but also of the nuances of business culture. Much depends on your own country of origin and which foreign country is hosting your global venture, but the entire process of recruitment and employment abroad is likely to challenge you with legal pitfalls and highlight cultural differences. For example:

• Headhunting is taboo in the UAE: under a law designed to restrict "job-hopping", employers have the right to prevent an employee who resigns from taking another job for six months.
• Indian cvs tend to include few personal details; by contrast, do not be surprised if a Greek applicant includes a certificate of health and a document confirming that they have no criminal record.
• Interviewees in Singapore are likely to write you a note after the interview thanking you for your time.
• The Chinese value modesty: do not mistake a self-effacing manner at interview for diffidence or lack of "drive". By the same token, they also largely prefer to fill in an application form than compose a letter extolling their own virtues.
• German cvs may run to 20 pages, neatly bound. It is customary to return them to failed applicants.
• Let an Indian team leader go, and you may find that half the team goes too: Indian workers can be more loyal to their line managers than to the company employing them.

ASK YOURSELF...
AM I READY TO RECRUIT?

Are you aware of the legislation and common practices of your host country as regards:
• Advertising of vacancies?
• Interviewing?
• The working week?
• Overtime?
• Minimum wage?
• Public holidays?
• Disciplinary action?
• Dispute resolution?
• Firing and notice periods?

Being culturally aware

Your management style abroad must include adapting to local conditions and cultures, and understanding different social norms and sensitivities. Business cultures around the world vary considerably in the way in which meetings are convened and conducted, negotiations are held, conflicts resolved, compromises reached, mistakes addressed, and decisions made.

TIP

PLAY IT SAFE
When in doubt as to the correct form of etiquette or business protocol in a situation, ask. Tact and sensitivity are appreciated everywhere.

Watching your language

Language can be a minefield when managing abroad. If you don't speak the language fluently, use your own interpreter for meetings. When writing to a client or supplier who does not speak your language, ensure there are no failures of communication by using a good translator. At the same time, learning a few words of your host country's language – even simple ones such as "hello", "thank you", and "goodbye" – is a courtesy worth extending. A good first impression may bring you business and make you friends. Show interest in your host country. Avoid making political statements and never, ever criticize your host country or boast about your own. Pay attention to how foreign colleagues dress, speak, act, and greet one another, and try to fit in with local norms.

CULTURAL ANTENNAE

"Face" in Eastern cultures
While Western management trends now emphasize the value of learning from mistakes, in many traditional Eastern countries "saving face" is a priority. Employees may be unwilling to admit to mistakes, while managers may avoid blaming other employees. As a result, mistakes may not be addressed at all. As a foreign manager you must be tactful and carefully explain, in private if possible, why mistakes are valuable in a learning environment. If shortcomings must be discussed in a meeting, be careful not to identify individuals with failure. While rarely effective in any culture, scapegoating is extremely counterproductive in the East.

Don't assume meetings or negotiations will be conducted in the same way – or with the same aims – as at home.

In some countries it is rude to launch into business discussions without exchanging pleasantries first. In others, meetings start with no preamble.

Check how direct you can be in meetings without giving offence – directness is considered aggressive in some cultures.

Getting it right in meetings

In some cultures business negotiations and discussions continue over meals and in after-hours socializing; in others, "shop talk" is frowned upon.

Steer away from jokes. What sounds funny in one country might be considered offensive elsewhere.

Rapid progress to using first names is common in some business cultures, but is not appreciated elsewhere. Keep your approach formal and stick to a surname until invited to use a first name.

Rising to challenges

As a global manager you will have a number of global, regional, and local trends, conditions, and situations to consider. Some of these may be commercial, while others may be political, economic, or bureaucratic, or relating to corporate social responsibility. The possibility of fraud, corruption, and counterfeiting may also pose risks and must be considered.

Assessing the risks

A risk assessment is crucial to any decision-making. For a small or medium-sized company, issues such as control, cultural fit, and image are crucial. Focus on good communication and relationships with suppliers, partners, and business advisers. In addition to red-tape complications and exchange-rate variations, particular risk areas are quality in offshored services or production, and management issues. Tales of exploited workforces and poor-quality products will damage your corporate image so communication and control are essential.

TIP

SELLER BEWARE

If you are a potential exporter, be wary of excessive interest in the technical specifications of your product from buyers, or repeated requests for prototypes, otherwise you risk being copied.

Setting up safeguards

Different cultures have different views of what constitutes corruption. Bribes are illegal worldwide, but breach of copyright is more complicated given the absence of a global copyright authority. This is often a source of conflict, notably in issues of patents, copyright, and counterfeiting. The more robust the patenting system in your own country, the better protected you will be, so patent and register everything – designs, trademarks, and local company and brand names – to clearly establish ownership. Ensure that you have an IP protection strategy in place, and restrict storage, access, and download rights on your network.

Key issues to watch

ON A LOCAL LEVEL

- Sourcing issues
- Skills availability/shortages
- Infrastructure/utilities
- Communication
- Quality/reliability
- Ethical behaviour
- Fraud/corruption
- Bureaucracy

NATIONALLY

- Financial instability
- Political instability
- Resource issues
- Environmental issues
- Regulatory issues
- Barriers to trade
- IP issues/counterfeiting
- Taxes and banking costs

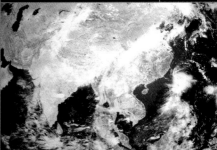

REGIONALLY/GLOBALLY

- Economic shifts
- Market profiles
- Financial instability
- Exchange-rate fluctuations
- Political instability
- Resource issues
- Environmental issues
- Climate change

Q IN FOCUS... COPYRIGHT
INFRINGEMENT – THE FUTURE

There is some evidence that in countries where copyright infringement is endemic, it may well diminish as the national economy develops and local expertise increases – because producing high-value local goods becomes more attractive, economically, than making cheap copies of foreign brands. China, for example, has long proved adept at imitating products, brand names, and packaging. But China's membership of the WTO has brought change, with the government encouraging legal action and creating more than 50 courts dedicated to ruling on IP cases. Chinese companies currently have approaching a million active patents of their own to defend, and have initiated a flood of lawsuits since 2003.

Considering ethics

Given the level and reach of worldwide integration and the opportunities and risks this brings, leadership and global governance have never been more necessary. The absence of a truly global system of governance and code of ethical behaviour can be problematic. The US Sarbanes-Oxley Act* is limited in its reach as it is only legally binding for companies quoted on the US Stock Exchange. The best guidance on good practice currently available is the UN Global Compact, which you can access via the United Nations website. This code of good conduct for business, established by companies and NGOs (non-governmental organizations), is subscribed to by several thousand member companies across some 100 countries. While it is voluntary and cannot be legally enforced, you may choose to make it clear that you require any global partners and subcontractors to recognize and adopt its set of core values on human rights, labour conditions, the environment, and anti-corruption.

*The Sarbanes-Oxley Act —
US federal law enacted in 2002, following a number of major business scandals, to set a standard for financial and accounting disclosure for US public companies. The Act was later "exported" to cover all companies listed on the US Stock Exchange.

Finding a way forward for "sustainable management"

Some of the most interesting views on the way forward for ethical, sustainable global business come from business thinkers focusing on CSR* and the problems of developing countries.

• A pioneer of corporate sustainability, Stuart Hart, SC Johnson Chair of Sustainable Global Enterprise at Cornell's Johnson School of Management, argues that global companies are particularly well placed to take the lead in identifying sustainable products to promote growth while helping solve the issues, such as poverty and climate change, that are leading to a backlash against globalisation.

• For Sumantra Ghoshal, founding Dean of the Indian School of Business in Hyderabad, the requirements of a global organization include that of a "new moral contract" with employees, based on recognition, respect, and motivation of the individual as a creator of value. His "transnational model" is characterized by its investment in local knowledge and training in cost-effective locations. Procter & Gamble and Unilever are prime examples.

• A uniquely motivational form of management is practised by Brazilian CEO Ricardo Semler, a WEF (World Economic Forum) Global Leader of Tomorrow. He runs his company, Semco SA, as an "industrial democracy" with no managerial structure (peer pressure acts as a natural restraint). Corporate financial information is completely transparent, and workers may opt for flexitime to achieve a work–life balance, elect whether to attend meetings, suggest their own wages, and choose their own IT equipment. This unexpectedly successful management design, which includes profit-sharing, has resulted in substantial productivity and growth and, perhaps predictably, notable loyalty towards the company.

*__*CSR__ — corporate social responsibility; how businesses take responsibility beyond any statutory obligations for the impact of their activities on society at large: on the local community, the environment, and the quality of life of their employees.*

Watching global trends

The global economy, representing some 200 countries across five continents and more than two dozen time zones, mirrors many different influences – some of which may have a substantial impact elsewhere. Stay abreast of political and economic developments worldwide. They may not appear to affect you initially, but may in time have a knock-on effect on the cost of your operations or the health of your markets.

Tipping the balance

In today's increasingly interlinked world, there are many examples of the effects of seemingly local events and crises spreading to quite dramatic effect. While a recession may start in just one country, the growing integration of the global economy can lead it to spread around the world. Losses resulting from the US sub-prime market crash in late 2007, for example, soon spread abroad – because US banks had sold on debts to financial organizations in other countries.

    The result was a crisis, job losses in banks, and a credit squeeze on borrowers in many other countries. The effects on the property market, businesses wishing to expand, and companies up- and downstream of them created a general economic downturn in the West. By May 2008 even major multinationals such as the Swiss chemicals group CIBA were blaming currency changes and surging raw materials costs for a decline in sales and consequent fall in profits. CIBA highlighted slow growth in NAFTA markets (the US, Canada, and Mexico) and throughout Europe, while Asian and Middle Eastern markets proved stronger – reflecting what is arguably the key economic trend of the early 21st century. The combination of financial market turbulence, major price inflation – notably for food and oil – and the slow-down of developed economies may lead to new calls for protectionist measures.

Recession-proofing your business

When newspapers start talking of economic slowdown, individual businesses report poorer than expected profits or redundancies, and consumers start spending less, these may add up to a coming recession. Your own firm may find that customers are taking longer to pay. Taking steps at this stage to ensure that you are better able than your competitors to weather a recession gives you the best chance of emerging from it ahead of the game.

Protecting your assets

Take these steps to lessen the effects of a recession:

Finance Review spending; cut costs where possible; liquidate unnecessary assets; chase unpaid bills; review loan conditions and renegotiate better deals where possible.

Marketing Enhance marketing to strengthen your position and show confidence.

Communication Communicate with staff to ensure best performance and maximum support; communicate with suppliers to ensure most favourable terms and conditions.

Confidence Remember that while recession is bad for some companies, it's good for others – some come out of it leaner, fitter, and stronger.

Index

Acknowledgements

Author's acknowledgements
Sarah Powell would like to thank
Tom Albrighton and Carol Fellingham
Webb for their interest, enthusiasm,
and suggestions.

Publisher's acknowledgements
Cobalt id would like to thank Neil
Mason, Sarah Tomley, Hilary Bird
for indexing, and Charles Wills for
co-ordinating Americanization.

Picture credits
The publisher would like to thank the
following for their kind permission to
reproduce their photographs:

1 Corbis: Don Mason; 2–3 iStockphoto.
com: Mark Stay; 4–5 Alamy Images:
Eightfish; 8–9 iStockphoto.com: Zlatko
Guzmic; 10–11 iStockphoto.com:
geopaul; 12–13 Dorling Kindersley:
Steve Gorton; 14 Alamy Images:
Interfoto Pressebildagentur; 15 (top)
Alamy Images: Russian Stock; 15
(bottom) Alamy Images: Bruce
Coleman Inc.; 19 (background)
iStockphoto.com: Manfred Konrad; 19
(foreground) iStockphoto.com: Julien
Grondin; 21 Corbis: George Steinmetz;
22, 23 (all) iStockphoto.com: Brendon
De Suza; 25 iStockphoto.com: Christine
Balderas; 28–29 iStockphoto.com:
Peter Jobst; 30–31 Dorling Kindersley;
33 Alamy Images: K-Photos;
36–37 Alamy Images: foodfolio;
37 iStockphoto.com: Elena Moiseeva;
40–41 Alamy Images: Derek Croucher;
48–49 iStockphoto.com: Tobias Helbig;
52 (top) iStockphoto.com: bubaone;

52 (bottom) iStockphoto.com:
Luis Carlos Torres; 56 (background)
iStockphoto.com: Russell Tate;
56 (foreground) iStockphoto.com:
Christopher Hudson; 59 iStockphoto.
com: Gary Woodard; 63 (chairs)
iStockphoto.com: Franck Boston;
63 (notepads) iStockphoto.com: Matjaz
Boncina; 63 (pens) iStockphoto.com:
Plamena Koeva; 65 (top) Getty Images:
flashfilm; 65 (centre) Corbis; 65 (bottom
right) iStockphoto.com: Jan Rysavy;
64–65 (bottom) Alamy Images: Steve
Bloom Images; 65 (bottom centre)
Alamy Images: Utah Images/NASA;
68–69 Alamy Images: artpartner-
images.com.

Every effort has been made
to trace the copyright holders.
The publisher apologizes for any
unintentional omission and would
be pleased, in such cases, to place
an acknowledgement in future
editions of this book.